Letters to
THE MODERN DAY CHURCH

Letters to THE MODERN DAY CHURCH

JASON DIXON

XULON PRESS

Xulon Press
2301 Lucien Way #415
Maitland, FL 32751
407.339.4217
www.xulonpress.com

© 2023 by Jason Dixon

All rights reserved solely by the author. The author guarantees all contents are original and do not infringe upon the legal rights of any other person or work. No part of this book may be reproduced in any form without the permission of the author.

Due to the changing nature of the Internet, if there are any web addresses, links, or URLs included in this manuscript, these may have been altered and may no longer be accessible. The views and opinions shared in this book belong solely to the author and do not necessarily reflect those of the publisher. The publisher therefore disclaims responsibility for the views or opinions expressed within the work.

Unless otherwise indicated, Scripture quotations taken from the King James Version (KJV) – public domain.

Scripture quotations taken from the Holy Bible, New International Version (NIV). Copyright © 1973, 1978, 1984, 2011 by Biblica, Inc.™. Used by permission. All rights reserved.

Paperback ISBN-13: 978-1-66288-044-5
Ebook ISBN-13: 978-1-66288-045-2

Contents

Preface vii

Chapter 1: Unto the Church of Competition, Write 1

Chapter 2: Unto the Church of Jealousy, Write 9

Chapter 3: Unto the Church of the Money-Driven, Write 15

Chapter 4: Unto the Church of the Superstar, Write 23

Chapter 5: Unto the Church of Lust, Write 31

Chapter 6: Unto the Church of Politics, Write 39

Chapter 7: Unto the Church of Deadly Traditions, Write 47

Chapter 8: Unto the Church of the Family-Driven, Write 53

Chapter 9: Unto the Church of No Effect, Write 61

Chapter 10: Unto the Church of Ungodly Leadership, Write . 69

Chapter 11: Unto the Church Who Named Themselves the Kingdom Gatekeeper, Write 77

Preface

God always has His ways of getting information into the earth that will benefit humanity. His only desire is to help us navigate through this life in a victorious way. In the book of Revelation, there are seven literal churches that God points out through the writing of John. Literal and spiritual implications were at the forefront of these writings both then and even now in the twenty-first century. Many issues, both then and now, have mirrored themselves down through history and must be made known to every listener that these things must be watched for and purged out of our lives. Starting out in Revelation, chapter two, you will find the church of Ephesus that over time had forsaken its first love. This church was praised for its hard work and distain of falsehoods and people who carried false titles. Still they fell away from the most important thing, which was God Himself.

Second, you see the church of Smyrna that would suffer persecution. They were admonished for strength that they did have and were reminded of the ones within the camp, who were wolves in sheep clothing seeking only to destroy and not uplift.

The third church was named Pergamos, and this particular church was called out to repent. There were some in this church, who were teaching false doctrines and causing many to sin through idolatry and sexual immorality. Repentance was needed to turn things around.

Fourth, was the church of Thyatira that were following false prophets, which is a huge issue. They were trying to do more and advance, but the tolerance of something God hated was an impassible wall.

The church of Sardis is the fifth church mentioned. They had fallen asleep and were in great need of an awakening. This church looked like it was alive but was really dead. They had become comfortable in their routine and did not realize that God was no longer in anything they were doing. They were more worried about the reputation they had among men than the connection that they needed with God.

Sixth, was the church of Philadelphia who endured the times patiently. They were holding on to the Word of God with all their hearts during very trying times. The promise of an open door was placed before them because of the faithfulness shown, and they were given encouragement to continue holding on.

The seventh and last church mentioned was named Laodicea, which we hear a lot about because they were neither hot nor cold but were lukewarm. The people that made up this church had amassed great possessions and had taken comfort in those things as the apex of life. It was not the apex of life, and the greatest missing link revealed was the well-being of the inner man which had been completely neglected and starved of any nutrition at all. Again, a call went out for repentance, which would become the only answer for real change.

It is with the inspiration of John's writing to the churches that this book is formatted for the modern-day era. Sin has been on full display in the modern-day church, and it must finally be addressed. It really is the *huge* elephant in the room that is not going to just disappear. The church has disqualified itself in many arenas because of the assimilation of inclusion and the loosening of our borders and standards. We as the body of Christ have been called to be absolutely different. "Come out from among them," says the Lord, "and touch not the unclean things" (2 Cor. 6:17). If the church is participating in all of the fleshly indulgences of the world, then it will become totally unproductive and lose the power to change and influence lives. There must be a major call for repentance that must ring out throughout our world. We must prepare now for the great awakening that God has been promised to us. The position and posture of the church in this hour is of the utmost importance. There will be no great awakening without this level of repentance.

Too many things have arrested the Church's attention as a whole, which is distracting from what is the most important thing—a true, pure relationship with God. There is a constant stirring of the pot to make sure that any type of healing or unity or even focus will be very difficult the way that things presently are. As you journey through the pages of this book, many things may touch you directly. Be ready for the "gut-punch" moments of "Wow, that's me." Other issues will touch somebody you know who has been or is currently in one of our multiple scenarios. The goal is a resurrection of hope and clarity that will lead people back to the true center of who we really are and why we are here. This will usher in the greatest awakening the world has ever seen!

Chapter 1:

UNTO THE CHURCH OF COMPETITION, WRITE

Church of competition, you may wonder why I'm writing to you. Many people feel that healthy competition is a good thing. Competition is often used to fuel some of the greatest sporting events, talent shows, and even family reunion cook offs. Having a great competitor often makes you better. You want to be better; you push yourself to be the best, so you study and train. What you, the church of competition, has to be careful of is when competition begins to tear apart the very fabric of unity God's Church was founded on. Competition has overwhelmed God's Church and has turned you against one another.

Competition in the church has become so rampant and pronounced that the church has not realized its focus has shifted off of God and on to outdoing the church down the street or in the same denomination. It has gotten so terrible that when one is questioned, the first questions asked are these: How many people attend your church? How big is your facility that you worship in? How many services do you have on Sundays? Are you in full-time ministry? Coming from a place of real concern and mentorship, these questions are welcomed because a helping hand and plan of action are present as well. Most questions asked in this manner place people almost in a direct position of being interrogated. The questions are not meant to uplift anyone but rather to simply pad egos. We are never to compare ourselves among ourselves.

Competition is defined as the act of competing; rivalry for supremacy, a prize, etc.: The act or process of trying to get or win something (such as a prize or a higher level of success) (Merriam Webster).

Competition has turned pastors, organizations, fellowships, and even brothers and sisters against one another. The lack of unity has weakened the body of Christ, as a whole, and has in turn played into the hands of the enemy. People with great value are often overlooked in a blatant attempt to hold the person back. No longer does the anointing on a person's life matter, only their ability to stay in a place that is comfortable for the agenda of others! Even if someone is gifted and could greatly help in situations, competition makes sure that they are not properly utilized and kept behind the scenes and out of the public eye. The question that needs to be asked is, do we really want to see God's kingdom in full affect or our own? Do we really think we can make it into heaven when we do all that we can to compete with and pull others down? Is the God of the Bible and His ways important enough for us to change?

> "And he said unto them, Ye are they which justify yourselves before men; but God knoweth your hearts: for that which is highly esteemed among men is abomination in the sight of God" (Luke 16:15).

There is no competition if there is no comparison. The rise of the social media platform has aided in this narrative as well. Everyone can see what the other is doing and oftentimes is doing nothing more than comparing themselves to what they see. The issue with this is that every seen platform is not functioning with equal resources, qualified people, or even up-to-date facilities. The level of biblical and secular study are worlds apart. The spiritual legacies and genealogies of a person play a major role as well. No two people are the same, so there is no need for competition. If you really look at it from its base, pride is the ultimate underlying cause. The oldest sin started the war in the first place and has placed us where we are today. Lucifer wanted to compete with God and be above Him. We are all aware that didn't work out too well for Lucifer and one third of the angels.

Many times competition is a learned behavior that is taught by those who came before. "Haters" is a word that I literally despise because it has sown the seed of competition and comparison time and time again. Those seeds have often grown into massive trees that provide cover and shade for all of those who harbor the same seeds in them. For the most part, no one is just sitting around plotting against you. No weekly meetings are held with you as the main agenda. Many of this is self-made to create a narrative and provides us with a story to tell. This only feeds a broken, dysfunctional cycle of constantly competing with a shadow of self-worth that can never be satisfied through outside humanity. It must come from within in order to be revealed on the outside.

God has told us that the harvest is ready to be harvested, but competition has slowed down the harvest process to a snail's pace.

Instead of sending people out to do the work of ministry, we proverbially sit on them. Why?

Consider this example: When a child goes to school, they are there to learn. A parent would expect for the teacher to faithfully teach and prepare their child for the next grade level. Each day brings a brand-new challenge of learning and new horizons to cross because the mind is being stretched to reach for things being introduced to it. We anticipate that the student would not remain in the same class for years on end. When graduation time comes, it is the honor of the teacher to see their students marching in cap and gown and going on to greater things. The student was taught and prepared and is now ready for every new challenge. The teacher can then focus their attention on the new group of students coming in and will start the process over again.

Competition has created walls inside of cities across our nation and even the world. Fast food restaurants understand that the more stores that they have in an area, the better it is for business. I have yet to see a church that can seat millions of people at a time. That tells me that there is room for more. The word territory should not even be named among us who say that we are carrying the gospel. How can you place boundaries between churches as if to protect territory? We must all remember that God has assigned voices and ears to hear them. You as one person cannot and will never reach everybody. The differences that God created us with was to match the diverse differences we see in our world. Follow the plan that God has set before you and run the race well. After that is the time to pass the baton on and take your rest. The harvest truly is plenteous, and masses of people need Jesus.

People are held back because of fear that they'll do better than where they came from. I thought we were on the same team. People are held back for fear that their spot or social position may be taken by another. Again, I say I thought we were on the same team. It has even gotten so terrible that phone calls are made to blackball and push people to the outside of the circle that they once ministered in. They were taught to believe and to fly, they were taught to step out of the boat and walk on water just like Peter, they were taught that they could do all things through Christ that's strengthens them; but as soon as they had the faith to believe and then stepped out on that faith, competition made sure that the infant dreams were suffocated before they had time to mature. I thought we were on the same team.

> "He also that received seed among the thorns is he that hears the word; and the care of this world, and the deceitfulness of riches, choke the word, and he becomes unfruitful" (Matt. 13:22).

In any competition, you have a winner and a loser. The loser always has the long bus ride home in total silence alone with their own thoughts of what they could have done better while thinking and wondering what went so wrong. I was only doing my best, giving it everything that I had. Many times, the loser never recovers from the loss that was endured. The winner earns the feeling of elation and happiness because of the win. Even a trophy is often given or some sort of symbolism to constantly remind you of your victory. In the kingdom, it is not the same. The loser is also left with this most disturbing fact when the loss comes from their own teammate.

In the kingdom we are all supposed to be on the same team, wearing the same color jersey and most importantly representing Jesus. The winner's elation at the hands of their own teammates only shows how far from God they really are, with the kingdom clearly out of plain sight.

It is in these times when we must understand that the team you're on is God's team.

Competition has caused many wounds throughout the years. People have served in capacities for years, giving of their time, finances, and emotional strength. Life sometimes takes people in different directions, and when these shifts occur, the gloves come off. Why? Phrases are used like, "If they were for you, they couldn't leave; and if they were against you, then they couldn't stay." I tend to disagree with this statement. If someone has served you, gave up things, sacrificed their life for your cause, they were with you. If two hands are in someone's back pushing them out the door, then eventually they will leave. The way people are treated oftentimes causes this effect to take place.

A battered wife will often stay in a relationship because of the love that she has for her husband. Though she is being battered physically, emotionally, and mentally, the pull to stay can be so strong. Her will has been broken; she has lost sight of who she really is. It is only when she comes to herself does she realize that she is a queen, royalty, and should be treated as such and should not settle for anything less. There is a real love that is tangible and can be attained. Many times, your passion can become your weakness and can be used against you because your heart is known. "Guard your heart for out of it flows all the issues of life" (Prov. 4:23).

As a child we were always taught to have good sportsmanship. Having played against friends who attended other schools than my own, we could always play hard and give it our all for our respective schools, and then when it was all over, we would all go out for burgers and fries and laugh it up. We put down all the hoopla, the cheers of the crowds cheering on their teams, the pounding of the hardwood floors, and just chilled.

Our heavenly Father instructed us to be as little children, and unless we are like children, the kingdom of God will escape us. I admonish you to use competition in healthy ways, but always remember the harm it will bring to you if you compete against each other. Our common competitor is our enemy and the only that!

Dear church leader, let me ask you a few hard questions.

1. Are you in competition with any other ministry leaders in the city?
2. Can you celebrate when another leader and ministry is doing well and comes into great favor in the area?
3. Do you celebrate the demise of other leaders in the city?
4. Do you get upset every time a new ministry is started in the city?

Remedy:

The saying has often been said that world stage is a pie, and there are enough slices to go around for everyone. We must all go back to God's original intention. John 3:16 says, "For God so loved the world that He gave His only begotten son, that whosoever believeth in Him should not perish but have everlasting life." This is the mandate of all who claim a kingdom connection to win as many as humanly possible to the Lord. This cannot be done if competition is present because people will always end up as collateral damage or simply overlooked in the turf war. This defeats our whole purpose, whereas the power of unity opens up so many avenues to new culture, ideas, and human perspectives which we cannot attain on our own.

Allow other people to teach you and be willing and open to learn. Come off of the island your ministry has been living on all alone, and you will be surprised of the forward momentum you will gain. These things all aid in the learning process of ministering to all people even as Christ did. If we want to win the world, then we must work together in order to do it. No one can do it on their own. Celebrating others takes absolutely nothing away from you or what you are doing. Please don't allow competition to pollute all of the good deeds you produce day in and out. Let's show our cities what kingdom maturity really looks like by having each other's back and helping each other up!

Chapter 2:

Unto the Church of Jealousy, Write

Jealousy is one of the oldest things in the history of creation and still is such a mystery as to why it affects as many as it does. It is the intrinsic nature of looking at others and what they have or have accomplished in life and being internally jealous about it. The issue is that jealousy never stays internal but always finds a way to manifest itself externally. In life, we are all given different situations in which we must navigate through because no two people are the same. If you really think about it, we were all born into different environments. Some environments lend themselves to better social or economic and even educational backing while others do not.

A family tree may be structured in a way that allows children to be raised by a village that runs two to three generations deep. On the other hand, many are born into impoverished conditions with little or no help anywhere in sight. The differences in society are often very difficult to understand by many prompting the question of one word: Why? Oftentimes the answer will be that life is simply not fair. That may seem like a hard statement to make, but nevertheless, it is still a very factual statement. The faster you realize this fact, you will also realize that you can succeed from any starting point that you have been given. With only one life to live, to continue wasting time is simply just not a wise move.

The word jealous is actually derived from a middle English word related to zealous, which means emotionally intense. It conveys a sense of emotional pain at someone else's good fortune.

The very root of jealousy caused the very first insurrection by you know who, Lucifer. He was so jealous of the ultimate position that God held that it engulfed him to the point that he lost everything. It was the first time that we saw this on full display but was surely not the last time. When allowed to grow, jealousy engulfs your life, your thoughts, and then your deeds. It is like a root system growing underground, invading every space and breaking through any foundations that are in its pathway. The end result is always thousands of dollars of damage and repair and don't forget the inconvenience. Jealousy never wants to be alone; it is very social, looking to draw support from those close in proximity.

The church of the living God is a living organism governed by people who have been put into place in different capacities. Like the natural body, all facets work in tandem as one in order to sustain life and continue to exist on this earth. Each organ knows the role that it plays in order to keep the function of the body going. You will never see the heart trying to be the lungs or the lungs trying to be the kidneys. The heart cannot leave its function to be something else because if it does, the body will die. All functions are necessary for life to continue. What the spirit of jealousy does is create a taste in your mouth for someone else's function, not understanding that they were not created for that function. You see the heart does not have the equipment to create oxygen for the body that is needed for life; the lungs do that. Jealousy overlooks these facts and the consequences of the facts and desires the position anyway. Jealousy would rather see everything fail than for the intended recipient to be celebrated in any way.

If you are a leader looking across town, seeing a beautiful edifice filled with thousands of people and you do not have all of these things, jealousy will soon be pulling up in your driveway and knocking at your door. If you fall into the trap, you will begin to look at the work you are doing as insignificant and minor. This way of thinking will begin to cause you to make decisions that will be detrimental to your ministry. This is a very dangerous pattern that all too many leaders have fallen into. This is a major warning not to fall for the trap. Jealousy will tell you that you need a new, bigger building, never mind the fact that you don't have the resources or the people to purchase a new building. It will simply be for show and tell. Jealousy will tell you that a bigger band is needed right now in order for you to keep up, again not counting the cost of the extra resources needed to facilitate such an addition. You create the persona of being big, even when you have not been equipped to do so.

You will quickly become a ministry that will be what I call showing and sinking at the same time. It is well known that on that faithful night when it sunk, music was still being played on the iconic Titanic. The winning look had to be maintained, even though soon the Titanic would be resting on the ocean floor. Think for a moment about all the lives that were lost on that night. History even shows us that if the evacuation was handled differently, many more lives could have been saved. It was a very sad ending to what should have been one of the greatest voyages in history.

Jealousy causes leaders to place unnecessary burdens onto the parishioners in order to keep up with the jealousy issues that have taken over their hearts. Hidden under the blanket of growth, many times jealousy is the driving factor. You must realize that the church across town may have a million-dollar donor who is financing the vision. They have the capacity to do things financially that you can't do, and there is absolutely nothing wrong with that. We are all on the same team! If you are winning, then I am winning because this is a kingdom movement. Remember who you are working for, God. The scripture plainly tells us that we have all been given different talents, and some of us have more than others. God knows the exact weight level that you can carry and will never give you more than that. He loves you and doesn't want to see you destroyed through ambition fueled by jealous undertones. Always remember that to whom much is given, so much more is required.

Jealousy is never satisfied with just having what another person has; it must find a way to diminish and take down the other person. It is literally never ending and has no bottom. Just like Lucifer, you will always feel the need for your throne, ministry, name, or platform to be higher than everybody else's. This is something to really think about while leading. One third of the angels were convinced by Lucifer to rise up against God. What kind of conversation did they have? What possibly could have been said to them? Whatever enticing words were used that ultimately worked, and in turn, they all got thrown out of heaven, never again to return to the positions that they once had.

Be extremely careful when a jealous person tries to convince you to come up against someone else. This is where you need to heavily question the motives and become mature in how to try the spirit behind a person. The throne Lucifer wanted didn't include the other angels; the plan was centered around him. Jealousy loves company but never splits the spoils with who it recruited. Lucifer did not care about the consequences or who it would affect; he just wanted the throne. He was jealous of the system that was set up in heaven. He was jealous of God.

Are we jealous of the ministry systems that we see when we look around? Are we convincing others to follow us simply so that we can get what we want? Is the kingdom the driving force behind the decisions that you are making or has the sin of jealousy entered into your hearts?

If it is the kingdom, then all involved will be edified and will be a benefit simply because God will be in it. How many more people will be destroyed because of a jealous leader? Stay in the building you're in until growth is necessary. If you can only afford local speakers for a conference, then continue to do that until other doors open. If the car you have runs and serves you, then continue to drive it until change comes.

We can't continue to be jealous, move on, and purchase things we can't afford or maintain and then turn around and label them as blessings. Remember one key thing, the blessing of the Lord adds no sorry to your life or ministry. God will always bless his people and provide for the vision He has given you. If it's not God's vision and will, then jealousy will always arise and pull something out the people who God has not ordained.

Ask yourself today, What is my function? If I am the heart, then let me pump blood throughout the body with everything I have and cheer on every other organ doing its job because without them, then my job comes to an end. It doesn't matter how strong I am; if another area of the body is weak, the whole body is ultimately affected.

Remedy:

Begin to celebrate one another and allow the strength in your area to provide life-giving nutrients to the other areas in the body. Check the internal motives of your heart and spirit. Be honest with yourself because you know how easy it is to lie to yourself. Don't be afraid of what you see or find out about yourself. When wrong motives are exposed, then they can be dealt with before any damage is caused. Allowing yourself to be spiritually cleaned out will leave you with an unexplainable liberty and clear vision for your life and endeavors. In the natural body, when your internal body temperature goes down, the blood from the extremities surrounds your vital organs keeping life protected. If there is an injury, blood will rush into that area to carry healing properties to bring a faster recovery time.

There is no room for jealousy in the body. Teamwork is the only way to really succeed in this life and in ministry assignments. Begin to surround yourself with likeminded vision people. People who are not afraid of the greatness that is in you will add to and cultivate who God has designed you to be in the earth in which we live. With limited time, we can't afford to spend our time being jealous; we should be working together as one unit in order to leave a legacy and pass on a baton to the next generation of excellence. You are unique and one of a kind. God has you here on purpose, and the world needs what is in you, so be you!

Chapter 3:

UNTO THE CHURCH OF THE MONEY-DRIVEN, WRITE

Money is such a powerful thing and at the same time is one of the most neutral things we have in our society. It is one thing that we all need to function in the earth. From the moment of our births, there are costs that begin to occur in our lives. Even our Lord and Savior Jesus Christ, when it was time to pay taxes, instructed his disciple to go down to the river side and retrieve some money out of the mouth of a fish to take care of the tax payment. Every nation under the sun has a form of currency in which they do their daily business. Although money is a neutral thing, the way that humans view money can take on many spirits and tendencies, causing great gain or great harm.

Many parents will push their children into sports or activities, and oftentimes, the children don't want to participate in just for the dream of being rich. Sadly, many times, moral values and upstanding ideologies are placed on the shelf for the chance of advancement. This behavior, of course, only results in layers of pain and emotional anguish. How many stories have we all heard about pertaining to a young talent receiving life-altering monetary gain and then ending up strung out on drugs, alcohol, and destructive living and often destroying the very career and source of the life-altering money they came into in the first place. While the money was flowing, everything was great, but as fast as they were praised and surrounded by friends, associates, and takers, is the same speed they used to walk away when the money was gone.

The art of handling money is rarely taught in schools, which is leaving many of our children at a disadvantage trying to navigate through a life where money is the main focus. Especially in these crucial times, we have to do a better job at preparing the next generation for what is to come in the area of finance.

Of course, this is not painting every church with a broad brush, but we have seen enough to know that the same model of financial malpractice has slipped into our doors. With the allure of monetary gain, cars, houses, and fine clothing, far too often moral integrity is placed on the shelf. Many pastors have forgotten the main focus of ministry and entered the race of keeping up with the Joneses. The jealousy and envy of the pastor online or across town has birthed pyramid schemes and fraud, which has landed many in jail. Once intoxicated with it, it is almost impossible to break free from its grasp. It can become likened to a drug which births a "by any means necessary" mentality. At this point, God is no longer leading the church because the thirst for money is. Many fail to instruct on the fact that unchecked financial practices will always invite unchecked morals and behaviors.

> "For the love of money is the root of all evil. Which
> while some coveted after, they have erred from the

faith and pierced themselves through with many sorrows" (1 Tim. 6:10).

Money obviously is not evil, but the love of money is very dangerous. This statement can be seen all throughout our daily lives in business, the political world, entertainment, and regular street life. From the highest white-collar position to the roadside merchant selling fruits, the main focus is bringing in monetary gain. Many were brought up to earn an honest living, but in this day and age, fast money has become the biggest trend. Quick money is sought, without any responsibility or maturity. Many have a sense of entitlement that things should be given and not worked for. We have all heard that things of great worth take time to achieve. It is the process of time that makes things great. The process provides strength and cohesiveness like the rebar that is found in any concrete road. You can't see it with your eyes, but without it, the road would fail to perform its purpose for being created. Foundational living builds a sure structure that will last.

Nobody wants what I call a popcorn or fireworks success model. This is where you pop up quickly and then fizzle out. Fireworks are so beautiful while traveling up into the night sky, but once they have hit their peak they just create a big bang and then disappear and fizzle out of sight.

The enticement to look bigger or greater than you really are, is the driving force behind the fast money life. Why go to work for forty hours when you can just work the street and get the same wage for four hours? The enemy has tricked many into letting go of the right thinking and embracing this feel-good-now concept. You don't have to wait for anything; you can have it now. With this tainted philosophy, people have turned to selling their bodies, selling drugs, cheating people, lying and stealing just to have the persona of doing well. They would rather break into your house and take goods that they did not work for to sell on the street for—you guessed it—fast money. Always trying to impress people who have no bearing on your life is never a good idea. The look of success in life to many is more important than the substance of life itself. They can be dead on the inside but as long as they look the part to others, that is all that is important to them.

Sadly, this ideology has found its way into the church of the modern day, and it didn't just start today. Greed has derailed many from what could have been tremendous catalyst in the end-time push for revival and world change.

> "And he went into the temple and began to cast out them that that sold therein and them that bought. Saying unto them it is written, my house is the house of prayer but you have made it a den of thieves" (Luke 19:45, 46).

It seems as if in this day and age, when it comes to the things of God, nothing can be performed unless a dollar amount is connected to it. Any talent that God has blessed you with will not be used for any reason unless paid for. Prophecies cannot be given to someone unless the prophetic word is paid for first. Musicians will bounce from church to church faster than a tennis ball at the Australian open, looking for the highest bidder. For twenty-five cents more per week and not even a phone call saying goodbye, you will join another band. The issue is the lack integrity and faithfulness to anything but the almighty dollar bill. Wild gifts are persons who do not even have a pastor or a church home. They are submitted to no one and desire no spiritual covering, who can hold them accountable and watch for their soul. They are simply just hirelings, roaming from place to place on the lookout for another monetary opportunity to come up.

Something has to change in regard to this very dangerous system that has been created and patterned by the next generation that is arising. In getting caught up in this vicious system, what we have done has priced God right out of the church. Many conferences/events are only deemed a success if a certain dollar amount has been achieved and not if anybody was actually changed, delivered or set free. Did anyone receive the Holy Ghost? Had any viable healings taken place? Were any of the demons that came to the service stirred enough by conviction to be cast out of anyone? These should be the most pressing questions being asked.

If money is the main reason for the gathering, then the service should really be dismissed right after the offering because that's all you really wanted in the first place. The enemy often uses the area of finances because of its importance and pivotal role in the building of the kingdom. You can't adequately build or advance without it. The excellence that needs to be put forth in our structures and presentation take money to achieve. God promises that His people will be blessed and prosperous. This is a twofold blessing that covers both the spiritual and natural aspects of our lives. Danger always hides behind the motives of the heart.

We have all seen the offertory portion of a service take up to an hour to be received while the preached word will take all of ten minutes to complete with no altar call at all. A guest speaker in a service will spend more time counting the crowd in attendance rather than feeling after the spirit in the room, all so they can prepare the pitch to the people for a big offering. The pitch usually goes something like this: I feel in my spirit that there is one hundred people in here that needs to sow one hundred dollars. I saw it in a vision on my way here from the hotel, and I know it's in the house. They will promise husbands, wives, boats, and so forth: whatever it takes to pull it out of the people. We might as well just hire an auctioneer to run the offertory period of any service. This may sound comical, but it is all too real. The Bible teaches us that God loves a cheerful giver and despises manipulative practices used to attain money. Anyone who gives out of the position of cheerfulness will blessed.

How did we get to point? Greed! We must change the narrative and motives of giving financially back to its original intent. God will open the heavens and pour out in absolute abundance on anyone following Him and obeying the financial principles at work. A right heart and motive will never be overlooked.

In many cases, leaders have added too much to the ministry's plate and now have to manipulate the people to keep the agenda floating. Always remember that God is never responsible for something that He did not ordain. Jesus said that they had turned His house into a house of thieves. There was no spiritual edification at all, just the gathering of people for an empty experience. We must return to the word of God in its simple purity.

> "Bring ye all the tithes into the storehouse, that there may be meat in mine house and prove me now herewith, saith the Lord of hosts, if I will not open you the windows of heaven, and pour you put a blessing, that there shall not be room enough to receive it" (Mal. 3:10).

Remedy:

We must all realize that we are working for the Lord. It is clearly understood that money is needed to make anything work well. It is understood that the workman is worthy of his hire. The question is this: do we even believe anymore that God can provide for us beyond our wildest dreams? If we did, then many of the systems we have created to lean on with our own understanding would begin to look like what it really is: manipulation. God is a provider and will always provide for His people. His word cannot return unto Him void. Being steadfast and unmovable in what you believe will put into motion a plan of the direction that you intend on going.

Major blessings in the hands of a novice will only cause trouble. You have to know how to live within your means. You will never be blessed if you continue to spend more than what you bring in. Discipline in the life of a person is principal thing. To whom much is given much is required; it is a great responsibility to carry great blessings. Seek the wisdom of those who know about the subject matter you're dealing with and who are professional. You don't know everything, so find help.

Chapter 4:

UNTO THE CHURCH OF THE SUPERSTAR, WRITE

I know that the world system is built upon the premise that everyone needs to be a superstar. Many have gone as far as selling out their very soul just to taste the sweet nectar of superstardom. It is an intoxicating phenomenon consisting of screaming fans, whirlwind tours, people willing to do just about anything just to have a chance to get close to you. Your name is always in lights and on every billboard because you are a superstar. The intoxication of being a superstar can become so compelling that it can mimic the very same traits of being addicted to drugs or alcohol.

In too many instances, the church has adopted many of the toxic traits of worldly systems. Human nature, otherwise known as the flesh, always wants to be worshiped. This is nothing new; it has always been a battle of the flesh against the spirit in this area of life. The arrival of the superstar in the church kingdom was very quiet. There was a time when God was actually the one who was being worshiped and adored. The people came to church for Him and Him alone, but as we have all seen, a major shift has taken place.

Instead of God being the superstar, leaders have now taken on that role for themselves. With the model that the world has provided, entourages have been formed with the leader as the king. There are armor bearers neglecting their own wives, husbands, and even children to tend to the leader's every need. In many cases, there is no appropriate balance, which in turn creates major issues.

How dare you allow a person to serve you more than they serve their own personal family? How many vacations, anniversaries, kids' sports events have been missed because of the pressure from the leader? This is the superstar syndrome in full effect.

Think about this for a moment: when the "glory" falls, you have enough strength to hold a microphone in your hand but not enough strength to pick up a towel and wipe our own forehead. You now need somebody to dress you and tie your shoes for you. What is wrong with this picture? The world prides itself on having all the lights on them. From the very beginning, Satan's main issue was that he wanted to be a superstar. He wanted his throne to be high above the throne of God. He wanted to be God, worshiped and adored, and until this day he is still trying.

> "How art thou fallen from heaven, O Lucifer, son of the morning! How art thou cut down to the ground, which didst weaken the nations! For thou hast said in thine heart, I will ascend into heaven, I will exalt my throne above the stars of God: I will sit also upon the mount of the congregation, in the sides of the north. I will ascend above the

heights of the clouds; I will be like the most High"
(Isa. 14:12–14)

Superstar syndrome is never satisfied and is always searching for new ways to top the last high or thrill. Remember this: God is no longer enough because pride and ego are now playing the lead role. We have seen this issue on full display in recent years. One wife is no longer enough to hold the superstar's attention, so women on the side become necessary. Many leaders are just not marrying anymore, not because of the lack of options, but to keep their options open at all times.

Of course, with superstardom comes a lot of, you guessed it, money. We all know that large amounts of money in the hands of the immature is a very dangerous thing. Money does give you options whether good or bad. You can buy anything you want, good or bad; travel with ease, whether good or bad; and also cover things up by throwing money at it. It has been said that whatever you are when you are unknown will only intensify when you are known. It is imperative that your heart and ways are clean before true elevation ever comes into your life. This will protect you from all of the enemy's devices and traps set to trip you up. We must remember that praise is a very powerful entity that should only be directed at the only one who can handle it—God.

Mainstream media has pushed ideologies to humanity, especially through our youth. Many beautiful women think that they are not pretty enough or thin enough because a magazine cover said so. These false realities are destroying the minds of anyone who allows the error to enter in. The end result is always weeks and even years of wasted time chasing that false reality. Men are doing everything in their power to look a certain way because a magazine said so. Social media tells us that life is valued by selfie likes, and we know that's just not true. False realities are all around us every day, and we must pray that we never succumb to them. The focus is so much on the outside that the inner part of a person is often forgotten. The real essence of who you are is lost. Once the outside becomes the focus, it becomes the enemy's playground. The reason this is so serious is the fact that God said He will not share His glory with anyone, including us. If we are not careful, we will become our own God, worshipping ourselves and wanting others to worship us as well.

A servant's heart is in no way a weak heart. It is actually the pillar of strength that the world needs. Silent strength has the fortitude of a thousand soldiers, and if God didn't illuminate the servant's heart, they would never do it themselves. Their focus and work ethic speaks for itself.

> Second Timothy 3:1–2 tells us: "This know also that in the last days perilous times shall come. For men shall be lovers of their own selves."

The self-love that many have has gone beyond the healthy stages into the self-absorbent levels in life. When everything becomes about you and the use of terms like "if it feels good just do it" or "I'm just doing me" is the main drive of your thought process, we have become our own gods. We have put the Creator on the back burner and only even think about him during times of trouble. I am quickly finding out that many people don't really want God; they just need Him, and there is a big difference between the two. These people are only around just long enough for God to fix their problems, and once the issue is fixed, then back out the door they go.

Superstars think that they are on top with no one to answer to but often forget that they are simply human and will always be in need of the Creator. Sampson in the Bible was a great example of this. He was, if not the strongest man to ever live, he had the strength of God on his side and oftentimes showed it for all to see. The superstar syndrome soon kicked in, causing Sampson to quickly lose his edge even when dealing with simple things. He started to choose things that he knew were forbidden for him to have. The superstar believes that they have no boundaries to adhere to. Always remember that small compromises always lead to big ones. Sampson went against his parents and any counsel and involved himself with a particular woman named Delilah. She conspired with the enemy forces to take Sampson down. He realized that he wasn't a superstar after all; it really was God's power all along.

Ask yourself the question: What kind of conversation did Lucifer have with the angels that caused them to give up all the glory and splendor of heaven for him? You see in order to become a superstar, you have to have followers. I wonder whether he offered them a position. Did he offer them kingdoms and regions? Or, did he offer them knowledge just like he did to Eve in the garden? Think about it, what Satan is offering you today is to make you feel like you're a superstar when he is the only one who wants the glory. You are just a pawn in his wicked games.

When you exalted by men, then men can also take you down. When the exaltation comes from the Lord, no man can change that. For many people in the public eye, the worst times of their life are when the talents they have depended on begin to fade, and the public that once praised them begins to ridicule them. The spotlight is not on you anymore, no one is calling your name, and the phone is no longer ringing. It is in these times that you find out who you really are, the real you that you have been hiding from for years behind the walls of superstardom. For this cause, many don't want to let go and go on playing many times causing injury and enduring the constant ridicule of the media and fan base.

In the athletic world, the best player on a team is referred to as the superstar. Oftentimes, the contracts that these individuals have handicap the team from gathering other talent around that player because of salary caps, and so forth. Because they know that they have the talent that's needed, in many cases, they become arrogant and develop the thoughts of "you can't make it without me." They demean people and talk to people like second-class citizens because they know that it will be overlooked as long as they can go out on the field and perform. If anything doesn't go their way, they threaten to leave and begin to call out ownership and coaching staff often never wanting to admit that it may be them that is the issue.

Because superstars have fans, the fans often get involved in any way that they can, mainly through social media, radio and talk shows, and so on. They speak their minds passionately, oftentimes not even personally knowing the person that they are speaking of. The fact is, all a fan wants to see is a performance. Give me what I paid for.

Remedy:

We have all heard the saying that there is no I in team. This holds true today because the only glory getter will be God. He will not share His glory with anyone, no matter how much you think you should be receiving some. Everyone around us has value and purpose. The strongest units are the ones who utilize every strength that is at their disposal. Every gift and talent comes from God; it does not even belong to us. We must give it back to him in every avenue that we can. People are gifts to be unwrapped to reveal the greatness that rests inside. Treat all people as you would like them to treat you, for this will always go a very long way.

Chapter 5:

UNTO THE CHURCH OF LUST, WRITE

The makeup of the human body is the most extensive of all of the creation on planet earth. The creation of man in the book of Genesis describes God carving man out of the dust of the ground and breathing life into His creation. He placed on the inside of man everything that he would ever need to grow and become. All knowledge and imagination of expansion that the world enjoys today was placed in mankind from the very beginning. Inside of man was woman, and when God saw that it was not good for man to be alone, He brought forth that which was hidden inside of man—woman.

Men and women were created with some very distinct differences that will never change. Whether in the animal kingdom or in the human race, the ways that female and male coexist is much of the same. Males were created as protectors and providers, while woman were created as nurturers. Woman were designed to carry children or the next generation that would keep the human race going forward. The very beautiful creation of God, like everything else God created, was being watched by the enemy and targeted. If you really think about it, all that the enemy has done is to take everything God created and created a distorted duplicate.

With more and more souls being saved and coming into the kingdom of God, we must understand that you can't miss something that you have never had (sexual encounter), but the fact is, many have had sexual encounters before their salvation conversion. So what do you tell them on how to deal with what they have experienced and what their body still desires?

Which brings us to the conversation of lust. It is God that created the internal sexual pull between a man and a woman. Sexual desires are totally natural but are only to be unlocked within the borders of marriage.

> "God blessed them and said to them, 'be fruitful and increase in number; fill the earth and subdue it'" (Gen 1:28).

The only way that this command could take place is by the man and the woman coming together in a sexual encounter to cause reproduction. This is the beautiful creation of God; yes, God created sex. Our bodies were designed to want and to enjoy sexual encounters. God in His infinite wisdom knew and realized the power of this creation and immediately placed it into the confines of marriage to create a protection for all involved, meaning the man, woman, and children who are created through sexual encounters.

Men are most often driven by what they see while women are driven by what they feel (emotions). You must remember that the enemy knows our attributes as well as our natural desires and proclivities. In knowing this, he has taking another shot at God by polluting what God designed with his own creation.

He created a feel-good society, and because he knows that you can't miss something that you have never had, he created ways through music and media to lure people into areas that many were not ready for. God never desired for mankind to be exposed to sexual behaviors prematurely. These encounters helped to form the wrong concepts of love, sex, even the body itself.

Unfortunately, many in this generation were introduced to sex through molestation as children and have been left to deal with something they should have never experienced. Many hold in the trauma and shame, causing emotional damage for years of their lives. They blame themselves for what took place, even though they were the victim. It changes the mind and produces behaviors which many simply call acting out. Nowadays, children and teenagers learn about sex on the streets and at school from their friends, resulting in warped views. Pornography is one of the largest-grossing industries in our country, capitalizing off of the sexual exploitation of both men and women. The church cannot stay silent any longer; we must step in and build a bridge back to the correct views of a God given gift.

The reason this subject is so prevalent is because over the years, we have seen a decline in marriage and many just choosing to remain single. Of course, in no way does marriage answer all of the questions of life. Also being single does not take away the internal drives that you have, which in turn, causes many to succumb to their flesh. Right now in the church world, the ratio of men to women is very upside down at least five to one. For those of you wanting to be married, it may seem like the choices are not plentiful. Many have simply given up on the process of companionship and marriage, and this is exactly what the enemy wants. It opens the door up wide for you to simply give in to your sexual feelings and do whatever makes you feel good. This behavior is often labeled as I'm just doing me. The layers of emotional damage that are occurring during these times are usually not seen until it is too late. The recovery can prove to be long and hard because there is still so much that we just do not understand about the human emotions and heart.

The church world has had a flurry of sexual scandals in recent years. Major leaders of churches and movements have found themselves embroiled and sinking in this sexual quicksand. Although many do repent and find restoration and healing, there are still those who would rather paint a picture of a weak gospel that does not have the power to keep you. The danger in this ideology is that the next generation is learning how to live by what is lived in front of them. If the leader/pastor can't live the life being preached and taught, then why would you expect the followers to be able too? This is the destructive norm being created and must be called out.

As a leader you are called to a higher standard and to whom much is given, much is required. If you do not choose to live right, then please move out of the position and allow someone else to lead. The litany of excuses for sexual moral failures have grown old and tired. The stakes are way too high, and the damage that is being done is too severe. The bar must be kept high in order for next generation to have a fighting chance. You must lead by biblical example in all areas. There are simply just too many examples of how unchecked lust will destroy anything it touches.

The rise of sexually transmitted diseases is at an all-time high. Unwanted pregnancies are steadily on the rise, which in turn, causes other issues. The abortion issue is one of the biggest battlegrounds right now, with most people refusing to examine the root cause of most terminations—sexual lust. There are so many consequences that simply arise due to the unchecked lust in a person's heart. Young women in college with grand ideas of life now have to change course and direction because of an unwanted pregnancy. Of course, we know that your life does not end if you find yourself in a situation, but it adds layers of pressure that many just can't deal with, such as the breakdown of the family and the separation of children from a place of stability. The road to achieving goals only gets longer and longer.

We must all understand that men operate by sight, which means to all the ladies who wear skintight clothing, the men are looking. They are not thinking about God at all if you are leading in a service or gathering, and every part of your figure can been seen. Men also have very active imaginations, and I can promise you that God is not being glorified. I know that everyone wants to look beautiful, but you have to keep this fact in mind. Beautiful and seductive are two very different things. The same can be said for the men. The new fad is to wear everything tight so that all of your parts can be seen. Let me let you in on a secret: We don't want to see that. When you put on your clothing, you know before you leave the house exactly who you are trying to entice, so please stop.

Because the eye gate introduces so many lustful images, pornography has become a major issue. It is the secret thing that happens behind closed doors. Both men and women suffer with this addiction, saying that it is an escape and that it's not hurting anybody. Actually, the main person being hurt is yourself. You are only kidding yourself if you believe that this vice will not find a way to spill over into your reality. What you see on a screen, you will soon want to experience in reality, not realizing that what you're seeing is a drug and alcohol–induced situation that those involved are trying desperately to escape from. Marriages are hurt and often destroyed because you desire your wife to become Sugar, Bubbles, and Strawberry. Your wife should not and will never become those women, and your mind will become captive to your own perversions.

The mutual attraction between male and female is normal. It is how God made you, and those feelings will never go away. You will even have people tell you to pray to God and ask Him to take them away. Here's a secret: He's not going to. We have to learn how to live and win in his area through the Word of God that will change our minds and ultimately our actions.

We are not trying to create a persona of perfection to the world. We are not dealing with robots but with living, breathing men and woman. They have to know that even though we are in church, the issues of humanity can still be there at times. The difference is that we have an advocate that is continuing to empower us and strengthen us to stand. Life will tell you that you deserve some fun, so just go for it; but if it is outside of God's plan for you, then you will be left unfulfilled and searching again.

If you think that you are strong enough to beat the odds, you are wrong. The saints used to always advise the youth to go out on dates in groups to prevent certain situations or temptations. Of course, I understand that if two people want something to happen, it will. Therefore, we must just educate the best way we can to save people from unnecessary things in life that only apply pressure and add heavy layers of emotional bondage that God never meant for you to ever have to carry.

The reason that the enemy tries so hard to get you to fall is because he understands that the one thing that separates us from God is sin. Lust is not on the outside; it is on the inside. Other things you can simply walk away from, but you can't walk away from yourself. You must look into the mirror and not ask but demand that a change be made to better your life. Things can change in your life, so please stop believing the lie that enemy is feeding you. God said in His word that "I wish above all else that you prosper and be in health even as your soul prospers" (3 John 2). Also he wants you to live an abundant life in every way, including sexually.

Remedy:

You can find your way back to God because He never has left you in the first place. He has promised to never leave you or forsake you. You have not done enough wrong for God not to love you. He knows everything about you and needs you to know that He loves you. His blood covers the good, the bad, and the ugly and will turn it all into strength that will launch you into the destiny He has designed for your life.

Cut off all access to your sexual vices by blocking phone numbers, emails, and social media accounts. Set up adult content blockers with your internet provider. You must do whatever it takes to break the ties because remember this is an internal fight. Question your motives for anything you are doing. Find an accountability partner that you can trust. Allow them to tell you the truth about yourself no matter how hard it is to hear. The spirit of God will lead by example and conviction. The difference between a pig and a lamb is that when a pig falls into the mud, it doesn't want to get out of it. A lamb, on the other hand, will feel comfortable and will look for any opportunity to get out of the mud and to get cleaned up. Sex does not have to be a taboo subject, just discussed and walked through in a mature way with mature people.

Chapter 6:

UNTO THE CHURCH OF POLITICS, WRITE

To the church of politics, I am so surprised that I even have to write to you. Why do we even have politics in God's Church, the Church that God set up on the principles written in the Bible and left for us to use as our ultimate guide?

The two major branches of government in the United States are the Democratic and Republican parties. In a democracy, there are different branches of government to provide a sense of balance to the country. To have a different set of eyes looking at situations should always be a good thing, right? Not always. The parties in our government are so divided right now that instead of galvanizing the country together, they are further dividing it. Lobbyists with deep pockets manipulate senators and elected officials in order to get their agenda across, even if it detrimental to the whole. The thirst for position, power, and influence often drive people into very dark places that much too often have a point of no return.

Why do we have to be different is the biggest question that needs to be asked. We have all seen that picking sides only destroys the middle. Think about that for a moment, and let it sink in. The middle of humanity and the soul encapsulating all of the biases rule the day. In a space where unity has been used for a trigger word for power and authority, the divide is becoming wider by the day. How do we not see what is happening? How do we not understand that our biases are like oil and water; they will never mix. So in order to have unity, compromise and understanding will have to take a giant step forward.

Let's key in on the word understand just for a moment. We can no longer be so quick to dismiss the experience and plight of anyone or any group. Our general humanity must return in order to achieve this. Several times throughout scripture, Jesus was moved with compassion, having a deep level of understanding of what was going on in the lives of everyone He encountered. The common thread of man is to simply live a comfortable life; to be able to provide for his family; and live out his dreams, visions, or goals. Why should the political shield block that? If at this present moment you were to take every human being on the planet, which is over 6 billion and place them in the state of Texas, a family of five would be able to occupy 6,085 square feet of living space. That means nobody should be trying to hold anyone back; there is more than enough room for everyone to prosper advance and do well!

We have seen political views bring such a divide in the Church to the extreme of stating that if you vote a certain way, you can't be saved or don't deserve salvation. The absurdity of these reckless views speak for themselves, but many have bowed at the altar of a political party and agenda more than the altar of God. Much of this process is based in idolatry and a sense of not wanting our choice to be the wrong one, no matter what has been presented to us.

The hardest thing to deal with for a person with a dream to fulfill is being trapped in the whirlwind called politics, which creates the dependence on someone else to allow your dream to come to life through the ladder that the system has created. You see, the problem with this ladder system is that man has control over how high you can really climb. How many times have you seen someone come into a company and begin to outwork those that have been employed there for years, not meaning to compete at all but simply operating in what they have been trained to do and being grateful for the opportunity that was given. Then the person simply finds out that the ladder only goes so high until man intervenes and pulls the rungs out.

If you are a dreamer, the political world will never work for you. You will always feel like a fish out of water, desperately longing to be returned to your God-ordained environment. The one thing that everybody needs to remember is that we will not live forever, which simply means that our positions will one day be filled by another. It is then in our best interest to pour out our lives into someone else.

The Church has adopted systems from the world, which are causing great division and hurt. There are hundreds of ideologies that have been created because of a battle for political supremacy. Factions and clubs have been designed to keep people out and in turn to keep others in.

There are invisible sets of rules and regulations to follow in order to get into certain arenas, and if you are not willing to follow those rules, you are deemed as rebellious. What is not being communicated to you is the fact that you will never ascend to anything or fulfill your goals or purpose if you remain connected to certain political factions. If you have ever watched or participated in any political process, then you know all too well about the campaign trail.

The political world is a place where for months on end, platforms are created for one candidate to totally run down every other candidate with a dream of making any kind of change to their city, state, or country. Millions of dollars are spent on television and radio ads digging up every ounce of dirt they can find on someone, to make sure that their reputations and names are smeared. It doesn't matter if the infraction happened in kindergarten, a way is found to spin the story. So much energy, time, money, and emotions are spent on making another candidate look bad. The funny thing is, the same people who you are now trying to destroy are the same people who have been helping your cause for years. They have sown all of their time, finances, and family life for the cause of someone else's vision. Nothing was wrong with the person as long as they were pushing your cause, but as soon as they put their name in the hat for promotion, everything changed. If they were so bad before, then why did you have them around for so long? It is amazing how quickly views can change when your personal agenda is not the focal point.

I will never understand why we preach faith to people, telling them to walk on water and jump over mountains, but then as soon as they actually get up and do it, then they are wrong and labeled a devil. It just doesn't make any sense. Let's call it what it is: politics. In the political world, the name of the game is to hold on to a position as long as possible and keep everyone else out. Politicians also have certain geographic areas that they cover as a mayor, senator, congressman, and so forth.

In the modern-day church, other pastors are not allowed to bring places of worship into certain territories because the area belongs to someone else already. It doesn't matter that maybe God has ordained that pastor to be in that area to reach a different group of people who maybe another couldn't reach. How can a whole city be yours? You can't be serious? You have cities with three million residents in them, and your church has thirty people. Yet you don't want any help in that city because God is going to send a revival and all of the three million, nine hundred, ninety-nine thousand, nine hundred, and seventy people will be coming to your church. With all that is going on in the world, the church needs as many soldiers on the ground as possible.

There is a saying that goes like this: if you continue to do the same thing the same way, you will only end up with the same results. This is the definition of insanity. Politics because of secret agendas hold progress back on purpose in many cases. You may know that change would bring great growth and a fresh perspective to everything involved but still go against it because of self-made agendas. To hold a title means nothing if you are not operating in the capacity of the said title. Have we become so engulfed in pleasing man that we can't clearly see the directives of Christ and His church?

Politics in the church has destroyed the minds of many dreamers. Many leaders and churches have become nothing more than spiritual abortion clinics. When a person walks through the door, there is life, dreams, and endless possibility. This only lasts until they are drugged with a selfish agenda, and the dream is destroyed before it ever had a chance, oftentimes leaving that person barren and empty. Many times after these situations, even when a new pregnant idea is birthed in the mind, because of the past trauma, sustained dream miscarriages often take place. This is how serious politics in the Church has become. When a minister backslides, we are very quick to say that they didn't want God or the truth but never stop to think about the closed-door conversations that they had with a bad spiritual leader. The emotional confusion that they wrestled with was because of the heart of loyalty that they had for their leader and the spiritual questioning in the mind as to whether they really heard from God. The long conversations with a spouse and children as to why the family is being treated in an unseemly way is another. This is a burden that no one should ever have to face or carry.

Even after a person is gone, the political world still feels the need to cast blame and throw stones in an attempt to "build" themselves up and allow themselves to be validated for what was done. Politics must also try to secure all of the surrounding leaders against a person as well, further isolating them from the circle that they were once involved in. The lobbyists in their lives will always undergird the political with praise for what was done simply because the positions that they have been waiting for are still supposedly safe. There is one crucial point that the lobbyists always forget. If a leader destroys someone for political gain, then why would you think that the same fate couldn't happen to them? They see many feel that it is okay to sit back and watch somebody else being wronged as long as it is not affecting them, but always remember that your turn could very possibly be next.

Put yourself into the shoes of the other person. How would you feel? How would you respond? How would you navigate through the land mines that have been planted all over? Always feeling as if every step that you take creates an explosion no matter how good of intentions that you have.

Remedy:

Dreamers, you have to keep on dreaming. Always follow our ultimate example, Jesus. While Jesus was walking on this earth, the political groups were all against Him. Isn't it ironic that Jesus didn't fit in and didn't even try to? He realized that He was here with a purpose to fulfill, and that was His father's business. Many times when you are on track with God, you will not fit in. This is not a license to become rude, but you must fulfill the call of Christ on your life. You must answer for the talent that God has placed into your hands. He didn't give it to you for you but for others. Someone else is depending on you to be exactly what God has ordained before you were even born.

Do not allow politics to sidetrack where you are destined to be. This is not an easy task because human nature always wants to be among the crowd. The applause of men and titles behind your name are often worth more to men than actually connecting to God Himself. Don't sit idly by while someone is being destroyed. Ask yourself the question. Am I my brother's keeper? Yes you are.

Do not allow yourself to be swept up in the political world and cause a miscarriage of destiny. God has ordained things for you that has no previous point of reference. This is the time when you will have to trust Him and embrace it. When you release the political, it can become lonely, but know that God is ever present. Do not allow your faith to be plucked away from you, hope to be snatched from your spirit, or vision to be stolen from your heart.

For loyal people, this can be tough because of how you are made up. You want so much for something to work that even in the face of terrible odds you continue to try to hold on. In your mind, you will continue to try telling yourself that it is not real or really happening.

In many instances it will take God Himself to command a shift and change that will shake you loose from the political vise grip.

"Lift up your head oh ye gates and be ye lifted up." The King of glory is coming in. God is taking back his church out of the hands of those who think that it belongs to them. His glory will not be shared with another. People do not belong to any one person; they all belong to God. He died and shared His blood for them. God is the one who called them before they were even formed in the womb. It is God who keeps them breathing and dreaming. There is only one King: King Jesus!

Chapter 7:

UNTO THE CHURCH OF DEADLY TRADITIONS, WRITE

The definition of tradition is the transmission of customs or beliefs from generation to generation; an inherited, established, or customary pattern of thought, action or behavior. Our literal world and diverse cultures are designed and cultivated by traditions from the food we enjoy with all the many spices and ingredients, to the way we wear our clothes with their eccentric colors and fabrics and the cut of a designer's scissors. From the many hairstyles we enjoy to the cars we cruise in and the music that's coming through that radio, tradition is at the root of it all. Although you could not choose into what traditions you were born into, they are still learned and are a part of your life's DNA. As we all know, life really is a journey full of wells of learning and experiences. Experiences were given to us as gifts to open up our horizons and have the opportunity to understand life and those in which we share the experience in a greater way.

With millions of people living on earth, it is of great importance that we do our very best to understand differences. It is the immaturity of a person or entity to believe that all culture must conform to their culture. Maturity will drive a person to go exploring into the realm of humanity which God created.

The subject of traditions must be added to any conversation if you ever mean to win people, yes all people, to the kingdom. The line that is often being crossed is the line between the gospel of Jesus and the earthly human traditions, which people hold so dear. There is a big difference between the two. A person should have to give up all of their culture in order to receive the gospel or be accepted. That would be creating a club in which all are not welcome. The question is what would Jesus do? Would Jesus welcome all cultures? I think we know the answer to that question.

Obviously, we live in a viral society where recently a preacher proclaimed that facial hair/beard was not a part of the ingredients of the anointing. Was this a gospel message or a culture message? The statement was made strictly out of a cultural background and was presented as gospel, which was wrong. It gives the impression that they are anointed and superior to others because they shave their faces, which has nothing to do with the gospel of Jesus Christ. We have to be so careful how we navigate these waters and always be willing to learn and not to be close minded.

Many times deadly traditions show up greatly in the local church where leaders have created a monument unto themselves instead of God. If anyone presents new ideas, they are labeled as a troublemaker or in rebellion. Deadly traditions often crush the spirit of the youthful thinker and by youth meaning new thinker. The power of a ministry is in the fact that it can live on beyond the leader. That those around the leader are being taught and processed and matured into a living organism called the local church.

The word change should not be a curse word in your church. Have you ever seen something great crumble because of the saying "This is how we always do it!" Tradition doesn't want to change, and many will even threaten to leave if any tradition or sameness changes. A leader who is not strong will often cave into the pressure of deadly traditions in order to keep certain people happy. This practice only continues to weaken the structure as a whole. Everything changes; it is a rite of passage to what is next.

The church cannot be the only entity on earth that refuses to change. In corporate America, change is understood in order to keep up with supply and demand. To stay as a Fortune 500 company, the best is needed—the best personnel, product, and resources. As fast as technology changes, people have to be in place to navigate all of the turns. The church always seems to be behind in these areas. There are too many leaders that simply should have passed the baton years ago.

The power of the position oftentimes can be intoxicating, leading to missing pivotal shifts and windows of opportunity. Traditions have kept ill-equipped people in positions that they should have long been dismissed from. Why would you keep someone in a position, who is not doing the job? If they worked with you at your place of employment, you would have fired them, but in the same situation in the church experience, we make excuses, again weakening the structure of the whole. We enjoy the best everywhere we go, and the church experience should be no different as far as the level of excellence being produced.

When you really take a big step back and look again many of the traditions, are there as fences or walls to keep people out and have created idols of worship unto ourselves? Jesus said if I be lifted up from the earth He would draw all men unto Himself. Who are we lifting up? If the focus is Jesus, then we can't allow our cultural differences to get in the way of allowing that to happen. The differences should exemplify the very image of God in the earth and unify all in the church for a powerful display of God's love.

Deadly traditions steal the option of the new. Who doesn't enjoy new things? I know God does. One of the greatest stories in scripture depicting this was the children of Isreal coming out of Egypt, who literally were set free by miracles, signs, and wonders after praying for freedom. But then, they desired to go backward into what they were used to at the first sign of adversity. Change can sometimes be scary because it is the embracing of the unknown, but as believers, we know our ultimate calling card is faith. We walk by faith and not by sight. Faith is the key the Bible says without which no man can please God, so we have to make a choice. Are you going to change and embrace new things or stay the same?

Blessings will often show up in different packages. We have all ordered from Amazon and have received a big heavy product in a tiny box or a tiny product in a car-sized box. That's the fun of opening every box to see what is inside. It's like having Christmas all year long, I can see why it can become addictive. Deadly traditions block out anything that looks or feels different causing major misses. Packages show up in different colors, shapes, and sizes. This is why having the mind of Christ is so vitally important. "Let this mind be in you which was also in Christ Jesus" (Phil 2:5).

Jesus came for the entire world. John 3:16 says, " For God so loved the world, that He gave His only begotten son, that whosoever believes on Him would not parish but have everlasting life." If God desires the heart and life of everybody, then the church is supposed to be exactly the same. Oftentimes, bad human experiences, wrong teaching, and cultural biases will close and shut down the mind, limiting the things God has planned and designed for His people.

We must, once and for all, break this stronghold. We must see how God sees, love how God loves, be as God is. Don't be afraid to break up the deadly traditions you know are present; and for those who know that the deadly traditions will never change, this is your confirmation of release. Following God with a pure heart is worth anything that is left behind. You will find a peace and spiritual liberty that surpasses all human understanding. You will see God!

Remedy:

One of the main words for this remedy is acknowledgment. The mind must be opened to the fact that deadly traditions are present and must be deconstructed. There are some things that simply are not Bible based. Don't be so stubborn not to look into these areas and deal with them. Any organizational infrastructure must be built in a way to last beyond the current leadership and culture. The message of the gospel doesn't change, but the methods of spreading the gospel must change in order to keep up with the ever-changing world around us. Leaders must create a tier system team where all of the responsibilities are not resting on the shoulders of one person. When it is a one man show, it does not represent power; it actually illuminates fear. This step will take trust and faith in those around you. After all, it is the job of every leader to empower, teach, and train those who follow them to one day serve in various capacities. It is the leader's job to listen and not just to dismiss every new idea presented to them.

There must be a realization that change is not bad. The creation of a team only makes you stronger, reaches further, saves valuable time and salutes unity. It's time for you to take a real inventory of your ministry or program. Are there people in positions, who shouldn't be? Are you worried that you're going to make a family unit in the church upset if change is made? Do you walk on eggshells every time something new is introduced to the ministry? Have you been threatened that if you change something, people will leave? Are you used to hearing, "This is how we've always done it"? These are just a few red flags that deadly traditions are present.

Don't limit yourself when we are serving a limitless God. Allow yourself to grow in grace, and you will find a renewed liberty and a restored joy of your salvation!

Chapter 8:

UNTO THE CHURCH OF THE FAMILY-DRIVEN, WRITE

The ministry always begins with a call, a very distinct pull on a person to take a step of faith and begin to seek out how they can affect the society in which they live. For many, a need has surfaced that may also cause concern that leads to a motivation to change the narrative of a city or neighborhood. The Bible lets us know that no man can build a house unless he first counts up the cost of building the house. The glaring questions must be asked. How much is this going to cost? How much manpower will be needed? How long will this take to build? These are all the fundamental questions that must be answered before you can even begin.

Many times as I drive throughout different you come across many unfinished structures. In most cases, they simply went over the allotted budget and did not have enough resources to finish up the job. When more available resources are again acquired, the job can be completed. In extreme cases, the building is lost to another builder who has the money to buy the assets from the bank. Counting the cost should always be the primary goal to make sure that you have enough capital to finish what you have started.

Ministry aligns itself to this form of thinking as well. Any person who starts a ministry must first understand that it is not just them who going into this venture but the entire family. Never forget that spouses and children are involved in any endeavor that you undertake. In many cases, a man will become a pastor, and his wife will become the first lady of something that, in many cases, she did not bargain for. That causes me to pause here to interject that before you choose a spouse, if you are considering ministry, a major conversation needs to be had to make sure that all are on the same page.

This is critical to the success or even failure of a ministry. If you love the ministry, and she doesn't love it, then two different directions will be established at the onset. Is she willing to travel when the need arises for ministry engagements, or would she rather stay at home? The first lady of a church is just like a mother in a home, a nurturer and caregiver. Does your wife even like people or like to be around crowds? Does she like to entertain and love on people? Don't get me wrong, there is nothing wrong if this is not a woman's cup of tea, but she should not be the first lady of a ministry. These attributes can't be faked because people pick up on it quickly. It has to be real and coming from the heart.

People feel what you can't even see, it is the way that God created humanity. If your wife lives for gossip and is a proponent of spreading gossip, then you're pretty much finished before it even gets started. People want to know that if there is an area in their lives that they have discussed with their leaders, it doesn't find its way to anyone else. There must be safety and confidence in knowing that the spiritual and natural wellbeing of a person is protected. She can't be the person feeding the piranhas who are just waiting for a meal. You can be friendly and kind with people, but you can't become common with everyone. You will never be able to be objective and minister from your spirit if you know everything about everybody. That is not called being concerned either; it is more commonly known as being messy. Nobody is perfect, but you must be aware of the attributes of a person that may not change with time.

When a church first is formed, in most instances, it is father (pastor), the mother (first lady), and the children (musicians). Many messages and Bible studies will be taught to just your family until increase comes and others become a part of the ministry. What this dynamic does from the very beginning is create a family circle that even as the ministry grows and prospers, the family is still the only one that benefits from the ministry. Everybody has heard the saying that blood is thicker than water. This statement does have its truth but, at the same time, can cause major issues if not handled correctly.

As a ministry grows and more skilled and qualified people are attending your ministry, there must be some room and opportunities that are available for these people. In most cases, those positions will be held by a family member. Many times, it is an under qualified family member who was plugged into a position because there was just nobody else to do it. Now that they have been doing it for a while and do not want to give up the prestige of holding onto the title, they do not want to give the position up. It makes no difference to them if they really don't know what they are doing, and there is someone else who can jump right in and run with it, they are still not giving in. Little Jimmy has played the keyboard since you started but only knows "Mary Had a Little Lamb" refuses to allow a skilled musician to take over, and Aunt Janet doesn't want to see Jimmy moved out either. Double standards are often present as well where sin is only sin for the congregation but not for the family members.

The pastor's office and the kitchen table at home are not very far apart at all. When a pastor leaves the church building, everybody goes in a different direction, but his family is coming with him. The balancing act now begins between saints, family, and the ability to make sure that the ministry is moving forward with excellence. Believe it or not, the pressure of trying to keep family happy can be heavier than the ministry itself. Pressure from home can many times taint the way that a leader sees things. He wants everyone to be happy and is often worried about the fall out. When family can't get their way, black mail or even threats of leaving the ministry or the withdrawal of financial support become normal. Wives will use the tactics of withholding themselves or just creating so much tension that the husband will usually give in.

Many loyal constituents have been casualties of the family-driven church. Knowing that people only belong to God, we all must understand that the church also only belongs to God. Life creates change at times, and people may not always be directly connected to you, and that should be fine. However, in most cases, it is not. This is why family-driven churches are held onto because the thought process is that at least the family won't leave. This usually cripples a church.

Change is a word that many do not like, but change is vital to the growth of absolutely anything. The fight against change only comes from people who have been doing something the same for so long that they are now comfortable. I have my special seat, I always say the announcements, I always sing the solo and so on and so forth.

God forbid that a visitor comes to the ministry and sits in your seat; everything must come to a standstill to rectify this travesty of disrespect. The main goal of reaching out has been lost in an endeavor to keep the little social club gathering at the size that it is. We are in control, and that's exactly how we want it.

With no checks and balances, family approves everything many times allowing the ministry to hemorrhage finances, never really having any real explanation to where the money is actually going. If questions are ever asked, you are instantly labeled as a devil and are against the ministry. Your intentions could be as pure as they can possibly get. At this moment, everything changes but not for the better. Once labeled, all efforts will now turn toward you and making sure that no one else has the same views that you do.

The feeling of alienation of members is always, in essence, the largest hurdle. The wall that has been created must come down. You have to be able to trust someone without your last name.

How long would you stay with a company that you knew was a dead end to your career, thus limiting your overall life? You always watch as the same circle of people get cycled around at the top without anyone else even being offered an opportunity. The only accomplishments ever celebrated are those of the family, once again creating a wall of petition. If an idea is given for growth or improvement, it is quickly shot down only to be picked up by a family member and then praised. If sin is committed by the family, then nobody needs to talk about it or else curses will fall and tongues will get stuck to the roofs of mouths. All bets are off, though, if a member sins. All of their business will be spread all over the church and called a mess. How then would you expect one to feel trying to serve under these types of conditions? In this kind of environment, gifts, talents, and any type of potential in a person are blown out like a candle in the night, by a leader who never intends to let your light be seen.

You must realize that control is often created by coming down on one person or family. It sends out a subliminal message to all others that the same treatment will befall you if crossed. People then immediately feel a need to stay silent in the midst of very adverse situations. Always remember that a broken spirit and will is the hardest thing to mend. It can keep you bond to things and treatment that in normal circumstances you would never tolerate. God told us that He has not given us the spirit of fear, but fear is one of the things that grips many in the pews, that is, the fear of making the leadership mad at you and bonds to be broken.

Many people have grown up in situations in which the father was not present. Real love was never displayed nor was a sense of normalcy. Leaders have taken the place of absent fathers and mothers. The church family has become more real to many than their birth family. To just drop people as a tactic of submission is just wrong. How can you use the love someone has for you as a weapon against them? If you don't do what the leader wants, then you are simply replaced and thrown out like yesterday's trash. Then when they are half destroyed, you have the nerve to say that they just didn't want God.

In an earlier chapter, we talked about a student being taught in school and advancing forward onto greater things. The church is not a spiritual cattle farm with everyone being branded to a certain owner. It should take on more of the attributes of an institution of higher learning. Push people forward because they have a destiny as well. These environments must be left in order to save both your soul and the souls of your family. Spouses and children are often the ones that have a front row seat to all of the damage that is caused. If not careful, they will begin to develop a distain for the church and the things of God. A place where love should abide and the example grace and family often take on the spirit of a haunted house at the state fair that many are afraid to go into. Children must see the purity of the church dynamic so that they can further understand God. If you are a parent, you need to make sure your family is in a place of worship that exudes this principle.

In any relationship, a separation causes some emotional pain. After you have been somewhere for many years, friendships and bonds have been made. A decision to make a change is a decision to let go of most of what has become your normal, even if it has been dysfunctional. Your mind will play games on you at times. You will say, "I wonder if the right decision was made." As a man, you will look at your wife and children that you are responsible for and ask God for leading guidance. At the end of the day, you will realize that the best decisions made are usually the hardest ones to make, and the end result is amazing peace.

Remedy:

You have to understand that the choices that you make for your family are number one. Remember this order: (1) God; (2) family; and (3) church. If you live your life in this order, then you will have an amazing life. I didn't say a perfect life but an amazing life. Life is not easy all by itself, and the last thing that you need is to be walking into a local war zone every Sunday morning and Wednesday night with the sign of a church on the front door. These are not churches, and that's why so many that pass through them are so damaged by the time they leave. The Bible tells us that you will truly know my disciples, my church, by the love that they have one toward the other. These are the places that you and your family must be found, a place where husband, wife, and children can all thrive the way God intended and where you are uplifted and strengthened for the journey. It is a place where you are empowered to go and fulfill the Great Commission that Christ gave to us all.

If the situation that surrounds you does not change, then you have to make a change. Enough time has been wasted. God said to remember to number your days that have been given to you. If not now, then when? If not you, then who? God did not call you into dysfunctional living but to a life of love, power, and a sound mind. Get up and shake yourself from your sleep and discontent. God has called you to fly, and who the Son has set free is truly free indeed. Decide today to take the step of faith into everything that God has called you to be.

Chapter 9:
Unto the Church of No Effect, Write

Matthew 5:13 states, "You are the salt of the earth. If the salt has lost his savor where with shall it be salted? It is thenceforth good for nothing but to be cast out and to be trodden under the foot of men."

This is such a powerful saying of a simple ingredient. Anyone that has cooked anything knows that salt is very powerful. Too much salt will destroy a meal and not enough leaves a meal not tasty at all. A master chef has mastered the balance of seasoning.

The church of God has been called to be salt, the absolute main ingredient of the earth. What is the church doing with the power that it has? Salt brings change, period; it changes things. If there is no change, then it has become useless. Think about it with me for a moment, and ask yourself the questions: Are you really salting your community? Does your community even know that you are there? Are you so worried about reaching the world that your adjacent city has not even been touched?

Many times because of a lack of focus and tying into many of the other subjects being tackled in this book, we have become of no effect. We are more worried about having the right look and persona rather than being effective. We have come up with catchy slogans like name it and claim it, blab it and grab it. We have told people to just run and shout as loud as you can, and after the shout, everything will just come pouring down. Many have finally realized that concept doesn't work just within itself; there must be major life changes. The embrace of worship and life choices must be pushed to the forefront. We are always telling people who God is getting ready to do something for but fail to address the position of the where and the why of their lives right now. We actually live in a principle-driven world and society. God created it that way on purpose so that it would be easy to follow the straight line. It is the lack of responsibility, maturity, and commitment to the process that has created this dynamic of no effect.

Change only comes when a decision is made. Until you get to the point of saying enough is enough, things will remain the same. Entertainment has taken over the platform/pulpit and has replaced the Church's true purpose and commission. If you entertain people into the house, then you will have to entertain them into staying. The church is not an amusement park filled with rides and cotton candy. The church is not a place to just medicate your issues for an hour and just go right back into the issues when you leave. If you continue to simply tell people to shout and refuse to marry the shout to substance, then you are doing a gigantic disservice to their lives and to their souls. Many ministries have become nothing more than a fast-food outfit where the food is bland and unsatisfying, always leaving you wanting something else. How do you engage someone to the point of change? How do you change the mindset of a generation?

Let's examine the very structure of the ineffective church or organization for the moment. Corporations are set up usually with this tier scale: workers, supervisors, managers, general managers, regional managers, vice president, and president. Everyone has a clear set of responsibilities that must be completed every day. There are weekly, quarterly, and yearly goals that are set in place and instruction given on how to achieve those goals. If the goals are not reached, then the ball starts rolling to find out why they were not met. Success can only begin if the weekly goals are being met before you can even think about the quarterly or yearly ones. The main thrust here is that everyone has to do their part, though differently, to achieve corporate success.

As I went down memory lane in my career I realized very quickly that in the corporate setting, I used to see my regional manager at least once a quarter. We would have meetings and discuss strategy to make sure my team was on track to hit every goal that was set.

When I survey the church world, I see too many instances of people who hold titles and are doing absolutely nothing to make sure the team is in a position to win. The thrill of the climb to certain levels is always invigorating, but after the arrival on that level, that is when the real works kicks in. You see the structure of the church world is very much the same as the corporate one; members, pastors, regional bishops, second presider and presiding bishop. When examining the two worlds, you will find that the Church lacks a tremendous amount of accountability on all levels.

The corporate world fears the consequence of the lack of productivity, while the church world does not. In the corporate world, if you do not produce, you are replaced in order to make sure that the weekly, quarterly, and yearly goals are met. The corporate world is not handicapped by the social pressure of pleasing and keeping non producers happy. We quickly celebrate this mentality when our favorite sports team trades or drafts a new player in order to get better. They are constantly looking for producers because they know championships are won with producers.

A liability or non producer is something that is working against the goal that is intended to be reached. If not dealt with, time will be the main thing being wasted and time is something we can never get back.

Many churches in an organization have never had their regional manager (bishop) ever walk through the doors of their church facility. They have no idea about the needs of the people and the churches that are in their care to cover. How does that even work? It looks good on paper to be able to say that you cover fifteen churches in a region, but most of the time those churches are usually on their own with no corporate strategy or help. Many pastors won't say anything because of fear of being labeled a troublemaker or too needy. The end result is a constant lack of effectiveness, major frustration, and eventually separation.

The corporate world makes sure that every branch on the tree is producing and has the tools to do so. Not much guesswork at all is involved; you just simply follow the pattern of success set before you. It has been tested and proven and worthy of being followed. Trainings, whether in person or virtual, are the norm to pass along vital information for success because they do not want you or the team you are over to fail. The view is that failure or success represents the whole, so failure is not an option.

It is time that those who hold titles are actually functioning effectively in those capacities, and if they are not, then change is a must. For the Church to regain its ability to salt the earth, the full capacity of everyone's responsibilities need to be in action again. At the top is where the tone is set for any organization. Winners always win is a mindset. Remember this: the mindset of the leaders is always passed down to the team and therein creates a winning precedence. As conduits of Christ, when someone comes in contact with us, they should feel and experience something different, just as salt changes the taste of anything it touches. Once it touches something, it never goes back to the flavor it was. God has called us to touch people and change the flavor of their life. The greatest compliment you, as the ministry body, can receive is that change has entered a life—a marriage restored, a wayward child changing for the better, an addiction being taken control of and broken, or the healing of someone's body. There are so many more life changes that can be listed; this is the purpose of our existence.

These changes will not come with a one-hit message, either. Change comes through a daily walk and discipleship. The right church family will play a pivotal role in the action of spiritual and natural growth. A village that surrounds a person or situation in love shows the amazing life that God has promised to all that will trust Him. Saltshakers move around and spread salt everywhere and on everything. We must begin to go again; we have sat still for too long, and the world has suffered because of it.

The right amount of salt enhances a meal to perfection and we are to do the same. Many times you will taste a food item and realize it just needs a little bit of salt. If you don't have any salt on hand, you will turn the stove down or off completely and go the store and get some salt because the meal won't taste right without it. You could just eat the food the way it is, but you know you would not be satisfied. Put the work in and enjoy the end result.

Right now the world is so bland because the Church has become comfortable with an unsalted pot of soup. If you realize this, turn the stove down or off, and go and get the salt that you need to finish the meal. Never be afraid to link up with a saltshaker. True saltshakers are only looking to enhance a kingdom agenda to empower those in the kingdom and to go after those in the family that just haven't found their way home yet. True saltshakers always offer just enough salt in order to make any situation much better and palatable for those that have to partake. Fake saltshakers will always allow self to get in the way, causing the situation to become so bitter that it can't be partaken of and has to be thrown away. In these cases, you have to start all over again, which is not always a bad thing. By starting over, you can take what you have learned and change for the better, making your life something tasteful for all who partake.

Remedy:

Your church should be known as a place that provides enough salt to cause life change and let down the wall and barriers that life issues have thrown in someone's way. I learned how to cook and season food from my parents. The skill was passed onto me, and now another generation is benefiting from that skill. Please take the time to learn from godly wise counsel. It is priceless and will teach you how to season a life and to save it both in the spiritual and natural. Never forget that we have to live this life out, and God promises a good life for us. Realize the ultimate purpose of your life is to glorify God and cause others to be affected for the better because of you. Let your light so shine so that men may see our good works and glorify the Father which is in heaven. If you remember that a soul is priceless, you will always handle a soul with extreme caution. A soul is a priceless commodity that belongs to God, bought and paid for with His own blood. The packing slip reads extremely fragile; handle with care.

Chapter 10:

UNTO THE CHURCH OF UNGODLY LEADERSHIP, WRITE

Our modern times have shown us that sound, mature leadership is now on the endangered species list and must be protected at all cost. The very definition of the word leadership is the state or position of being a leader and the action of leading a group of people or an organization. It is the leading of people who validate the severity of this discourse. People inherently need someone to follow in every area of life. Countries have presidents, sports teams have coaches, companies have chief executive officers, and churches have pastors. The leadership role must have certain characteristics in order to translate growth and health into the lives of those being led. Let's list just a few qualities:

They have a humble disposition;
They do not tolerate wrongdoing;
They are honest (integral) and open; and
They protect the people being lead.

> (Matt 18: 6) "If anyone causes one of these little ones—those who believe in me—to stumble, it would be better for them to have a large millstone

hung around their neck and to be drowned in the depths of the sea."

The human race in intertwined by a social tapestry which lends to the fact that some people will go off track by the influence of others. There is no reason to think that each individual will not be held accountable for his own sin, but it is also clear that those with influence bear a much greater responsibility. This is the premise that many leaders are not taking serious enough, which is causing a watered-down ripple effect on God's people. The truth of the matter is that many are simply looking for any excuse to live the lifestyles they are choosing. Being a leader should not be an excuse one can use for their behavior.

An elder must be blameless, faithful to his wife, a man whose children believe and are not open to the charge of being wild and disobedient. 7 Since an overseer manages God's household, he must be blameless—not overbearing, not quick-tempered, not given to drunkenness, not violent, not pursuing dishonest gain. 8 Rather, he must be hospitable, one who loves what is good, who is self-controlled, upright, holy and disciplined. 9 He must hold firmly to the trustworthy message as it has been taught, so that he can encourage others by sound doctrine and refute those who oppose it. (Titus 1:6–9)

There has been an all-out attack on the integrity of ministry and the spiritual space. We are not ignorant of where this attack is coming from and have to contend for the faith of ourselves and others because lives really do depend on it.

> (II Corinthians 2:11) "Lest Satan should get an advantage of us: for we are not ignorant of his devices."

The very integrity of leadership has been compromised to the point that many people have lost faith in it. We know that not all leaders are the same, but it always seems as if the bad ones receive all of the media attention. The sin and questionable dealings of leaders have taken center stage in the kingdom. As the book of Titus stated, leaders must be blameless and without reproach. Many of the leaders today parade their sins and indiscretions in the face of all and actually dare anyone to address or confront them. They use their platforms to explain their sin instead of finding a place of repentance. The worst part is that scripture is twisted, and grace is used as a blanket for unrepented continued sinful practices. This has created a form of godliness and has muted the power of God in many cases.

Warnings of manipulation practices must be brought to the forefront in order to save people time and pain. Ungodly abusers will use the very same tactics as any other abuser. The trick is to place the blame and shame onto the abused. Statements like, "If you really loved me, you would cover me" will be used. "We are all the same as humans" is another popular saying used to excuse the lack of the higher level of responsibility that a leader must possess.

> But we have renounced the hidden things of shame, not walking in craftiness nor handling the word of God deceitfully, but by manifestation of the truth commending ourselves to every man's conscience in the sight of God. (2 Cor. 4:2 NKJV)

> Instead, we have renounced secret and shameful ways. We do not practice deceit, nor do we distort the word of God. On the contrary, by open proclamation of the truth, we commend ourselves to every man's conscience in the sight of God. (2 Cor. 4:2 BSB)

For the ungodly leader to think that there is not a price to be paid for their actions is delusional. The seeds planted today will produce the harvest of the future. If sin is normalized by leaders, then the church member doesn't have a chance. Why are so many concessions being made for ungodly leaders? That question must be answered. For fellow leaders, could it be that you keep your mouths closed because you don't want to ruffle any feathers and be canceled by an ungodly culture? Is the chase to get to the proverbial top more important to you than an actual change in the life of a believer? To continue to turn a blind eye to what you know is blatantly wrong reflects a deeper issue of the heart. Now in speaking to the pew member, could it be that you have chosen to remain under ungodly leadership to appeal to your own sinful ways? Or is it to ease your own conscience and allow you to feel okay or just not as bad with your own ungodly actions? It's time to turn on the searchlight and check the issues of the heart.

> For the time will come when people will not put up with sound doctrine. Instead, to suit their own desires, they will gather around them a great number of teachers to say what their itching ears want to hear. (2 Tim. 4:3 NIV)

> For the time will come when men will not tolerate sound doctrine, but with itching ears they will gather around themselves teachers to suit their own desires. (2 Tim. 4:3 BSB)

To endure sound doctrine clearly lets us know that everything that you hear will not be pleasing to your flesh. Endurance speaks to longevity, maturity, and responsibility, just to name a few. Church culture has definitely moved away from these concepts, and we are seeing the full reflection of it in life's mirror. Something has to be done to reverse this dangerous trend. It will not be a popular message to the masses, but remember that Jesus already warned of this truth.

Clearly, here the power of choice is put on display. As much as the ungodly leader is responsible for the actions of their lifestyles that does affect those around them, there must be a level of responsibility laid at the feet of those who stay under them. Sound doctrine and a standard of living must be chosen by the pew. We all understand that what is in the heart will rule your life. The heart has to be guarded at all cost for out of it flows all of the issues of life. Ungodly leaders are well equipped and have studied human behavior and trends, which allow them to exploit damaged people. Keeping people broken allows them to easily be deceived and manipulated.

Many today are being led by carnal desires and continue to feed those carnal desires, only making it more difficult to hear and respond to sound teaching. When you enter environments of sound teaching, there will always be friction against those carnal sinful ideologies and desires. Sound teaching is designed by God to separate you from sinful practices. It is not for the comfort and complacency of the hearer. It should challenge your inner man to change and place the sinful nature under subjection—not to celebrate it.

Sin destroys everything that it touches, and we cannot allow ungodly leaders to minimize this truth. Lives are literally on the line because of the choices being made after being influenced wrongly.

Ask yourself these questions:

- Does your leader challenge you to change your sinful lifestyles, or do they continue to make excuses for it?
- Does your leader use grace as a blanket to cover up a continued sinful lifestyle?
- Is your leader involved in yearly scandals that always have to be explained away?
- Does your leader twist the scriptures in order to validate continued sinful practices?
- Does your leader demonize every person who dares to question the moral efficacy of their life?

These are all very serious questions that need to be explored and really answered truthfully. The goal is supposed be a life that is conforming to the life of Christ Jesus and ultimately making heaven our eternal home. Sin will always stand in the way of this process and must be elevated back to the level of being extremely dangerous to anyone who involves themselves in it.

Remedy:

You cannot be afraid to excuse yourself and your families from such places. Sometimes the greatest mistake made on life's journey is staying in the wrong place too long. This can create toxic norms in your life, which can cut off future ambitions and endeavors. There is no curse that can be placed on a person who makes the decision to escape from a toxic environment. The mental games used by ungodly leadership are demonic and very destructive. The Bible teaches us to do everything decently and with order, so how you depart is very important to the rest of your journey allowing the blessing of God to continue to flow even in hard situations. If the leader is not following Christ, then you shouldn't be following them.

As a pastor, I have instructed my congregation that if you see me cheating on my wife, committing willful sin, disregarding any sense of a moral compass, while being accountable to no one, you should leave my church and find a leader who is following God. It really is that serious. With eternity hanging in the balance, don't take any chances with your now or your then. Take the time to pray and too fast before connecting to a leader. Do not join a church just because it has great amenities. The integrity of the leader will create the culture of the church. What's in the head will always be found in the body. Choose wisely!

Chapter 11:

Unto the Church Who Named Themselves the Kingdom Gatekeeper, Write

In John 10:16, Jesus tells us, "And other sheep I have, which are not of this fold: them also I must bring, and they shall hear my voice; and there shall be one fold, and one shepherd."

It is always astonishing to see the levels of organizational structures that actually have named themselves the kingdom gatekeepers. Believe it or not, this premise is rooted in the spirit of pride. Let's examine this further by examining the life of our Lord and Savior Jesus Christ. When Jesus came to the earth the assignment was very clear.

> "For the son of man is come to seek and save that which was lost" (Luke 19:10).

Jesus Christ was very open in sharing the gospel of the kingdom with anyone that would listen. He was never condescending in His approach or mission. When Jesus called the disciples into duty, He promised that He would make them fishers of men. Any wise fisherman will tell you that you must use different methods, depending on the type of fish that you are trying to catch. Some species respond to color, others respond to size or scent. Whatever the case, the target is the deciding factor.

The gatekeeper title is nothing new to any society because in Jesus's day, the scribes and Pharisees were the main characters. They were the religious group who believed in their own minds that they were the only ones who were right, and anything that had to do with God had to be run through them. They challenged Jesus at every turn, trying to keep him out of their circles because his teachings ruined the stranglehold that they had on the people. He presented spiritual truth and freedom for all people, while their teachings pushed many away whom they deemed unfit. When the scripture says there is nothing new under the sun, it is spot on. Today, once again, we are seeing these ideologies on full display.

The number one thing should be the saving of souls and people coming to know God, but we have seen different. There are great awakenings happening all around our country and the world. Great prayer meetings and worship experiences are springing up on college campuses and church campuses where twenty-four-hour worship is taking place. As we all know, most college campuses behind the scenes are filled with sex, drugs, and elicit parties. Anytime a college campus turns into a prayer command center, this should be celebrated. Instead what we are seeing is the opposite. Instead of celebrating the good, the true heart and intentions of many people are on full display. Self-proclaimed gatekeepers have barricaded the door of anything godly unless sanctioned by them. It is 100 percent opposite to the approach that Jesus took. So many have forgotten that they themselves at one point were totally lost in need of a Savior.

1 Corinthians 6:11 says, "And such were some of you: but ye are washed, but ye are sanctified, but ye are justified in the name of the Lord Jesus, and by the Spirit of our God."

When this becomes our central theme, then we could never get caught up with a gatekeeper mentality. We must also examine the psychology of the people or groups being attacked by self-appointed gatekeepers. The question is why anyone would want to be a part of your group after they've experienced all of the nasty attacks and condescending narratives you have painted against something that is not filtered through your platform. It's a twisted way of thinking to think that you can attack people and then turn around and think that they will become receptive to your platform or anything you have, as a matter of fact.

There is a very real issue with most "saved" people who nobody wants to talk about. We spend so much time talking about how long we have been saved. You will hear things like, "I've been in the way for twenty years" meaning I've been in the church, living for God for twenty years. Most will wear it as a badge of honor, but this as we all see is becoming an issue. Let me explain, so we can have clarity. This is found in

Matthew 20:1–16:

1 For the kingdom of heaven is like unto a man that is an householder, which went out early in the morning to hire laborers into his vineyard.

2 And when he had agreed with the laborers for a penny a day, he sent them into his vineyard.

3 And he went out about the third hour, and saw others standing idle in the marketplace,

4 And said unto them; Go ye also into the vineyard, and whatsoever is right I will give you. And they went their way.

5 Again he went out about the sixth and ninth hour, and did likewise.

6 And about the eleventh hour he went out, and found others standing idle, and saith unto them, Why stand ye here all the day idle?

7 They say unto him, Because no man hath hired us. He saith unto them, Go ye also into the vineyard; and whatsoever is right, that shall ye receive.

8 So when even was come, the lord of the vineyard saith unto his steward, Call the laborers, and give them their hire, beginning from the last unto the first.

9 And when they came that were hired about the eleventh hour, they received every man a penny.

10 But when the first came, they supposed that they should have received more; and they likewise received every man a penny.

11 And when they had received it, they murmured against the goodman of the house,

12 Saying, These last have wrought but one hour, and thou hast made them equal unto us, which have borne the burden and heat of the day.

13 But he answered one of them, and said, Friend, I do thee no wrong: didst not thou agree with me for a penny?

14 Take that thine is, and go thy way: I will give unto this last, even as unto thee.

15 Is it not lawful for me to do what I will with mine own? Is thine eye evil, because I am good?

16 So the last shall be first, and the first last: for many be called, but few chosen.

As you can see in Matthew 20, many had a great issue with the payment method, and this is still a huge issue today. The celebration of being saved seems like it is no longer enough for many people. We are comparing ourselves, even in the kingdom experience. The longer that you walk with the Lord should produce levels of maturity simply because of time. Time in any relationship should cause growth and the fruit of productivity. A longer relationship with God was never meant to place you in a different category, allowing you to now look down on those just arriving or, as we call them, "babes in Christ."

Maybe the bigger issue with self-appointed gatekeepers is that of true authentic deliverance and freedom. Has the gatekeeper really been freed from their past? Throughout your walk with the Lord, there should be a laying down of immature actions and spiritual childlike behavior. Many seem to be stuck watching babes in Christ find their way into maturity and almost have the need to penalize them for every stumble that they encounter. Maybe it is because the gatekeepers' true desire is to still participate in what they have supposed to be delivered from. New people to the kingdom love the Lord as a babe; they have not given up what you have, they have not sown what you have sown, and they have not labored in the kingdom like you have. This is understood but it's because they are new. Many saints forget that they had time to grow, mature, and to get life issues right. How many missteps did it take for you to finally beat your vice? How many of you still struggle with a vice? When you look at yourself, it is very hard to try to push other people out of the circle or slam the door in a seeker's face.

Have you realized yet that you need to drop the gatekeeper act and allow God to be God? Please stop using cultural, organizational, or reformational expressions of worship to divide and to deem something as not being real in the sight of God. Doing this only continues to place on display your spiritual immaturity and continues to harm the body of Christ on a whole. Anything moving in the direction of God should be celebrated, considering the alternative. The job of every believer is to love people like God does.

> John 3:16 says, "For God so loved the world, that He gave His only begotten son. That whosoever believeth in Him should not perish but have everlasting life."

Remedy:

It is time to take down all of the hurdles and obstacle courses that have been set up simply to appease manmade structures and not God. Everyone needs to take a very good look at yourselves and make sure that your Lord and Savior is Jesus Christ and not your reformational institutions. Many have followed flawed structures of thinking and practices for years simply because someone said so and have never researched or searched scripture for yourself. The goal is to get people to Jesus, for He is the only one that has saving power. Nothing should ever get in the way that. Pride must placed to the side in order to accomplish this task. I know that it is hard to face the fact that maybe some of the ideologies that you have held so near and dear to your heart are flawed in nature. If you're afraid of losing friends and associates over your changes, then that would be a normal human response. I guess the greater question is: How important is a soul really to you?

About the Author

Jason Dixon was born and raised in Toronto, Canada. Being a husband and father of three, family is a big part his life's journey. After moving to the United States at the age of eighteen with his family, the call of God lead him to Houston, Texas, to attend Bible college in preparation for working in ministry. In 2016, in a God-ordained succession from his father, Bishop Aquilla Dixon, he assumed the role as the senior pastor of The Power Of God Ministries in the beautiful city of Port Charlotte, Florida. He also leads a dynamic crusade/mission ministry called Jason Dixon International Outreach Ministries (JDIOM) that travels the world preaching the wonderful Gospel of Jesus Christ and assisting in many humanitarian needs. Helping people win in life is the ultimate goal; let's win together!

www.ingramcontent.com/pod-product-compliance
Ingram Content Group UK Ltd.
Pitfield, Milton Keynes, MK11 3LW, UK
UKHW022216230426
12048UKWH00016BA/880